BRIGHT IDEA BOOKS

KENDRICK Lamar

by Martha London

a Capstone company — publishers for children

Raintree is an imprint of Capstone Global Library Limited, a company incorporated in England and Wales having its registered office at 264 Banbury Road, Oxford, OX2 ?DY - Registered company number: 6695582

www.raintree.co.uk
myorders@raintree.co.uk

Text © Capstone Global Library Limited 2020
The moral rights of the proprietor have been asserted.

All rights reserved. No part of this publication may be reproduced in any form or by any means (including photocopying or storing it in any medium by electronic means and whether or not transiently or incidentally to some other use of this publication) without the written permission of the copyright owner, except in accordance with the provisions of the Copyright, Designs and Patents Act 1988 or under the terms of a licence issued by the Copyright Licensing Agency, Barnard's Inn, 86 Fetter Lane, London, EC4A 1 EN (www.cla.co.uk). Applications for the copyright owner's written permission should be addressed to the publisher.

Edited by Claire Vanden Branden
Designed by Becky Daum
Original illustrations © Capstone Global Library Limited 2020
Production by Melissa Martin
Originated by Capstone Global Library Limited
Printed and bound in India. PO 864

ISBN 978 1 4747 8743 7

British Library Cataloguing in Publication Data
A full catalogue record for this book is available from the British Library

Acknowledgements
Quote Source
p. 25, line 6–7: Adam Fleischer. "Here's Why Kendrick Lamar Is Embracing Being a Role Model." http://www.mtv.com/news/2289446/kendrick-lamar-role-model. 11 March, 2019.
Photo Credits
Alamy: Erik Kabik Photography/MediaPunch Inc, 26–27, Photo 12, 8–9; AP Images: Chris Pizzello/Invision, cover; iStockphoto, jjwithers, 7; Newscom: Frank Micelotta/PictureGroup/Sipa USA, 5, Jerry Perez/PacificCoastNews, 19; Rex Features: Bebeto Matthews/AP, 21, Matt Sayles/Invision/AP, 16; Shutterstock Images: Christian Bertrand, 24–25, 30–31, Ga Fullner, 14–15, Joe Seer, 11, Kobby Dagan, 12, 28, Twocoms, 23
Design Elements: Shutterstock Images

Every effort has been made to contact copyright holders of material reproduced in this book. Any omissions will be rectified in subsequent printings if notice is given to the publisher.

All the internet addresses (URLs) given in this book were valid at the time of going to press. However, due to the dynamic nature of the internet, some addresses may have changed, or sites may have changed or ceased to exist since publication. While the author and publisher regret any inconvenience this may cause readers, no responsibility for any such changes can be accepted by either the author or the publisher.

CONTENTS

CHAPTER ONE
BEST RAPPER ALIVE 4

CHAPTER TWO
GROWING UP 6

CHAPTER THREE
MAKING MUSIC 10

CHAPTER FOUR
MAKING A DIFFERENCE 22

Glossary 28
Timeline 29
Activity 30
Find out more 32
Index 32

CHAPTER 1

BEST RAPPER Alive

Red lights flash across a huge stage. The bass thumps. Then everything goes dark. Suddenly the lights come up. Fire blazes on the sides of the stage. Kendrick Lamar is in the middle of it all. He's playing Madison Square Garden in New York City, USA. Thousands of people are in the crowd.

Lamar's song "DNA" begins. It is about the hard times black people face today. It is also about how black people need to stick together. Lamar has been called the best rapper alive.

Kendrick Lamar uses dancers in some of his performances.

CHAPTER 2

GROWING Up

Kendrick Lamar was born on 17 June 1987. He grew up in Compton, California, USA. The area had a lot of **violence**. He saw two people die when he was a child. This event has shaped his whole life.

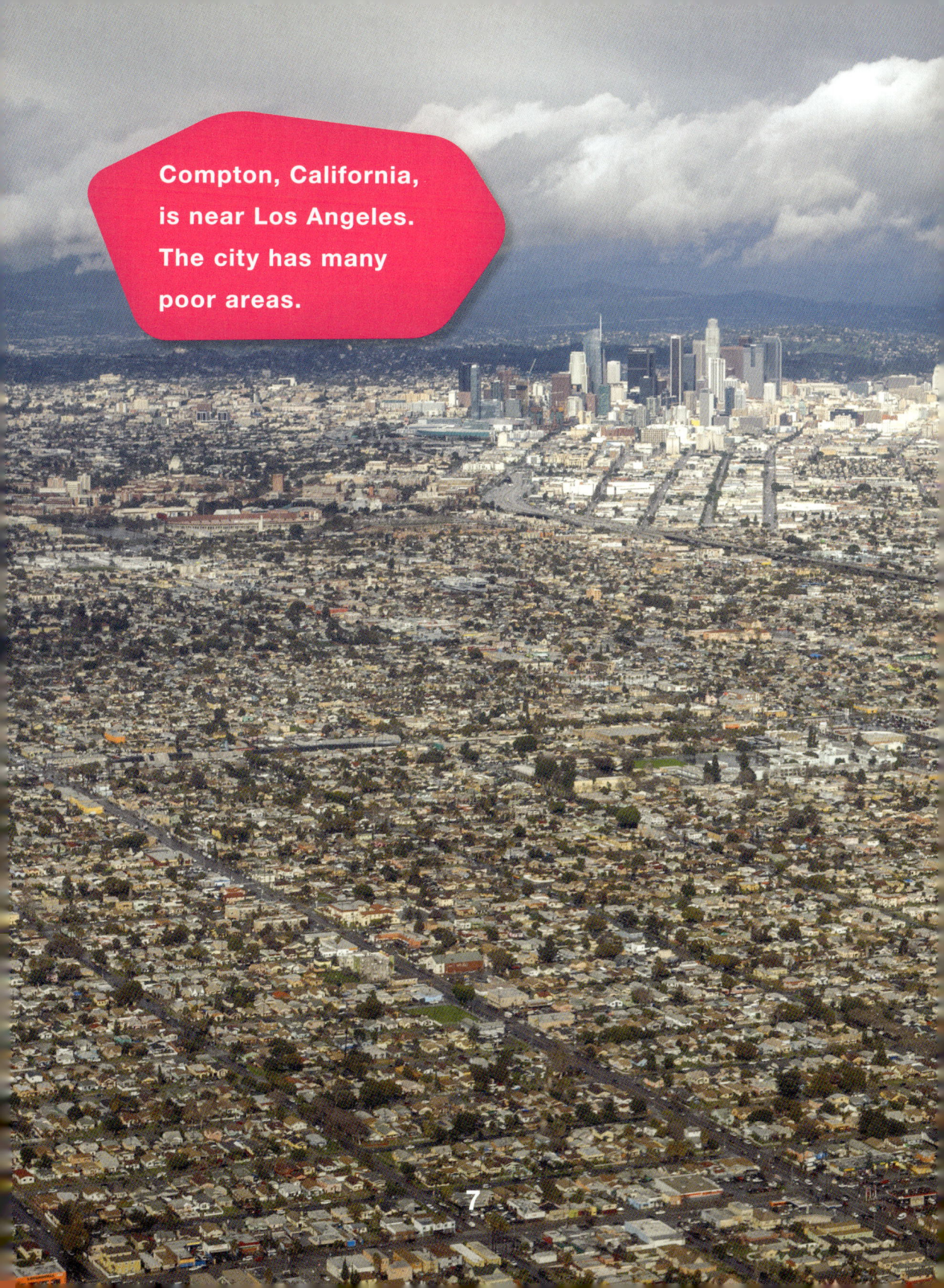

Compton, California, is near Los Angeles. The city has many poor areas.

Tupac Shakur (below) was a popular 1990s rapper. Lamar says that Shakur's music has been the greatest influence on his own music.

Lamar grew up listening to music. He listened to Michael Jackson and Marvin Gaye. He enjoyed Tupac Shakur's music. Lamar loved music. He began rapping when he was 8 years old. He called himself K. Dot.

Lamar stopped going by the name K. Dot in 2010. But his friends still call him Dot.

CHAPTER 3

MAKING Music

When Lamar was a teenager, one of his teachers at school showed him **poetry**. He started writing and did not stop. Lamar liked that he could write down his feelings.

Lamar gained attention across the country after his single *good kid, m.A.A.d city* came out.

Lamar had a stutter when he was younger. He said music helped him overcome his speech problems.

Lamar continued to work on his music. A **record label** signed him. He made many **mix tapes**. Then he made his first album in 2011. It was called *Section.80*. It was about life in Compton.

Lamar's second album came out in 2012. It was called *good kid, m.A.A.d city*. People loved it. Lamar shot to fame. He was **nominated** for seven **Grammy Awards** in 2013. One was for Best New Artist. Another was for Album of the Year. Lamar did not win. But many more people learned who he was.

Lamar went on to make three more albums. He made one almost every year. Most artists take nearly two years just to make one album.

Lamar was nominated for many more Grammys. He has won Grammys for Best Rap Song and Best Rap Album.

In 2017 Lamar won six times at the MTV Video Music Awards.

Lamar won a Grammy Award for Best Music Video during the 60th Grammy Awards in 2018.

Lamar's music continued to top the charts. He won many awards during the 2018 **NAACP Image Awards**. One was for Outstanding Album. Another was for Outstanding Song.

Lamar was nominated eight times for the 61st Grammy Awards. He won for Best Rap Performance in 2019.

Lamar was very busy in 2018. He made new music. He also **produced** the **soundtrack** for *Black Panther* with Anthony Tiffith. Lamar rapped on the soundtrack too. The film was a big deal. It was the first Marvel film with almost all black actors. Lamar was proud to work on it.

Lamar co-produced the *Black Panther* soundtrack with Anthony Tiffith (right). Tiffith owns the record label that signed Lamar.

Later in 2018, Lamar won the highest honour. He was awarded a **Pulitzer Prize** in music. It was the first time a rapper had received the prize.

MAKING HISTORY

Only classical or jazz artists had won the Pulitzer Prize in music before 2018. Lamar's award made history.

Lamar received his Pulitzer Prize on 30 May 2018.

CHAPTER 4

MAKING A Difference

Lamar has done a lot. But he doesn't want to just make music. He wants his music to make a difference. Lamar believes music can build bridges between people.

Many people relate to Lamar's songs.

AN IMPORTANT JOB

Music can help people get through hard times. Lamar's music has made him a role model. He thinks it is a very important job. He has previously said that being a role model "means everything to me".

Lamar writes music that he believes will have a positive impact on others.

Lamar is proud of where he came from. He wants to help kids from Compton succeed. He has given money to after-school programmes. He also gave $50,000 (£41,660) to the music department at his high school. He wants music to help others like it helped him.

Lamar continues to make a difference through his music.

GLOSSARY

Grammy Awards
an awards show that honours the best artists in music

mix tape
a collection of songs

NAACP Image Awards
annual awards given to people of colour in the areas of music, film and television

nominate
to suggest that a person might be the right one for a job or an award

poetry
a type of writing

produce
to guide the creation of a project from start to finish

Pulitzer Prize
a global annual prize that honours outstanding work in a specific field

record label
a company that makes music

soundtrack
an album for a film

violence
rough physical force

TIMELINE

1987: Kendrick Lamar is born in Compton, California, USA.

2011: Lamar's first album, *Section.80*, comes out.

2012: Lamar's second album, *good kid, m.A.A.d city*, comes out.

2018: Lamar is nominated many times for the NAACP Image Awards.

2018: Lamar is nominated for eight Grammy Awards.

2018: Lamar co-produces the *Black Panther* soundtrack.

2018: Lamar becomes the first rapper to win a Pulitzer Prize for music.

ACTIVITY

WRITE YOUR OWN RAP

Kendrick Lamar's home town influenced much of his music. Write a poem/song/rap about your home town. What problems do you see that you want solved? What inequalities do you see? What should be done to solve or improve them? Now think of how art or music changes your community. If you don't see change, think of ways in which art or music could be used to start a conversation about change.

FIND OUT MORE

Feel inspired to learn more about music? Check out these resources:

Books

Create Your Own Music (Media Genius), Matthew Anniss (Raintree, 2017)

Recording and Promoting Your Music (I'm in the Band), Matthew Anniss (Raintree, 2014)

You Can Work in Music (You Can Work in the Arts), Carolina Walker (Raintree, 2019)

Website

DK Find Out!: World Music Day
www.dkfindout.com/us/more-find-out/special-events/world-music-day

INDEX

Black Panther 18

Compton, California 6, 13, 26

"DNA" 5

good kid, m.A.A.d city 13

Grammy Awards 13, 14, 17

K. Dot 9

Madison Square Garden 4

NAACP Image Awards 17

poetry 10

Pulitzer Prize 20

role model 25

Section.80 13

Shakur, Tupac 9